Gender, Peace and Security
Women's Advocacy and Conflict Resolution

Fredline AO M'Cormack-Hale

Commonwealth Secretariat

Published by the Commonwealth Secretariat
Edited by Tina Johnson
Designed by S.J.I. Services, New Delhi
Cover design by Tattersall Hammarling & Silk
Printed by Hobbs the Printers, Totton, Hampshire

Views and opinions expressed in this publication are the responsibility of the author and should in no way be attributed to the institutions to which she is affiliated or to the Commonwealth Secretariat.

Wherever possible, the Commonwealth Secretariat uses paper sourced from sustainable forests or from sources that minimise a destructive impact on the environment.

Copies of this publication may be obtained from:

Publications Section
Commonwealth Secretariat
Marlborough House
Pall Mall
London SW1Y 5HX
United Kingdom
Tel: +44 (0)20 7747 6534
Fax: +44 (0)20 7839 9081
Email: publications@commonwealth.int
Web: www.thecommonwealth.org/publications

A catalogue record for this publication is available from the British Library.

ISBN (paperback): 978-1-84929-074-6
ISBN (e-book): 978-1-84859-128-8

Foreword

During the 1990s at least 10 Commonwealth countries were engaged in armed conflict or war, the impacts of which particularly affected women and girls. Peace agreements were eventually reached in many of these countries, with women playing a critical role in bringing the conflicts to an end. In recognition of both war's adverse effects on women and women's important contributions to peace and security globally, the United Nations Security Council unanimously passed resolution 1325 in 2000. UNSCR 1325 urges governments not only to protect women from all forms of violence during armed conflict but also to support women's participation at all decision-making levels for the prevention, management and resolution of conflict as well as expand their role in peacekeeping operations. It enjoins member states to develop national action plans (NAPs) or other national-level strategies to facilitate implementation of the resolution.

The Commonwealth is committed to meeting international obligations including UNSCR 1325 (and subsequent UNSC resolutions on women, peace and security), the Convention on the Elimination of All Forms of Discrimination against Women (CEDAW), the Beijing Platform for Action and the Millennium Development Goals. The Commonwealth Plan of Action for Gender Equality 2005–2015 calls on governments to promote women's full, equal and effective participation at all levels and stages of peace-building processes including formal and informal negotiations and agreements. It encourages the mainstreaming of gender equality into the training of peacekeepers, disciplined forces and law enforcement personnel to ensure appropriate codes of conduct. It also advocates for the implementation and monitoring of UNSCR 1325 through the adoption of NAPs in Commonwealth member states.

The political and democratic situation of member states in conflict and post-conflict settings is reviewed through the Commonwealth Ministerial Action Group (CMAG). Since its creation by Commonwealth Heads of Government in November 1995, CMAG has reviewed as part of its agenda: Belize, Fiji, The Gambia, Guyana, Pakistan, Sierra Leone, Solomon Islands and Zimbabwe, and has made recommendations for appropriate intervention and action. In addition, the Commonwealth Secretary-General has deployed Special Envoys for preventive democracy and conflict resolution through and the Eminent Persons Group as reflected in the 1991 Harare

Declaration, the 2009 Trinidad and Tobago Affirmation on Commonwealth Values and Principles and other key documents.

The participation of women in conflict resolution, peacemaking, peace-keeping, peace-building and post-conflict reconstruction has expanded across the Commonwealth. Some 28 Commonwealth countries have contributed troops to peacekeeping and peace-building operations around the world, among which Nigeria ranks the highest in contributing female troops followed by Ghana, South Africa, Bangladesh and Rwanda. In 2007 India deployed the first all-women contingent – a Formed Police Unit – to serve in the UN operation in Liberia. Since then three more all-female UN police units have been deployed from Commonwealth countries: Bangladeshi in Haiti, Samoan in Timor-Leste and Rwandan in Sudan.

At least 33 Commonwealth countries have adopted national gender policies for women's equality. Other countries – including Botswana, Grenada and the Maldives – have drafted national gender policies that are awaiting adoption, while most countries in the Pacific region have just commenced the process. Some countries have introduced other equality measures; for example, Sri Lanka has a Citizenship (Amendment) Act that guarantees equal rights for women and men. Yet only 5 of the 33 countries worldwide that have developed NAPs on UNSCR 1325 are in the Commonwealth: Canada, Rwanda, Sierra Leone, Uganda and the United Kingdom (though others, such as Australia, New Zealand and South Africa, are in the process of doing so). This calls for more pointed action particularly as there is little evidence of women's increased participation in formal peace-related negotiations and decision-making committees or bodies.

This book aims to contribute to ongoing efforts on peace management. It elaborates women's engagement in peace and security and their effective contributions to conflict resolution and peace-building processes. It further examines women's efforts in the adoption of NAPs across Commonwealth countries and provides case studies from Commonwealth countries that have adopted NAPs. In addition, it uses paragraphs taken from UNSCR 1325 to trace the progress that selected countries have made in attaining the resolution's goals.

Ultimately, the adoption of NAPs fosters the institutionalisation of gender mainstreaming and equitable practices at all decision-making levels and helps states – whether they are affected by conflict or not – to fully co-ordinate national efforts to meet the requirements of UNSCR 1325. Robust implementation would entail integration of UNSCR 1325 into national policies and training programmes if its objectives of prevention, participation, protection and relief and recovery are to be attained. Monitoring and evaluation in accordance with key indicators identified in the NAPs themselves is critical and penalties for non-compliance should be regulated and made effective through all structures and systems of governance, at all levels and across all sectors. Commitment to budget allocations is essential in making this a reality.

Ms Esther Eghobamien
Head of Gender
Social Transformation Programmes Division
November 2011

Contents

Abbreviations and Acronyms

DDR	disarmament, demobilisation and reintegration
FRELIMO	Liberation Front of Mozambique
ICTR	International Criminal Tribunal for Rwanda
LRA	Lord's Resistance Army
MDGs	Millennium Development Goals
NAP	national action plan
NGO	non-governmental organisation
PoA	Commonwealth Plan of Action for Gender Equality 2005–2015
RPF	Rwandan Patriotic Front
UNAMSIL	United Nations Mission in Sierra Leone
UNSCR	United Nations Security Council resolution

About the Author

Fredline AO M'Cormack-Hale is an Assistant Professor at the John C. Whitehead School of Diplomacy, Seton Hall University in South Orange, NJ, USA where she teaches courses in International Relations and African Economic Development. Her research interests include gender, development and democratisation in post-war states, with a focus on Sierra Leone.

1. Introduction

The recognition that conflict disproportionately affects women is well documented in the conflict and peace-building literature. Given the rise of internal conflicts in particular, women's non-governmental organisations (NGOs) and concerned governments worked together to place this issue, as well as acknowledgement of the part women play in conflict prevention and as advocates for peace, on the international agenda. The adoption of five UN Security Council resolutions (UNSCRs) dealing with women, peace and security – 1325, 1820, 1888 1889 and 1960 – was an attempt to meet the call for more nuanced understandings of the various ways in which conflicts affect women, to provide greater protection for women in conflict situations and to ensure that women are included in all aspects of peace-building and conflict resolution processes. In addition, the Commonwealth Plan of Action for Gender Equality 2005–2015 (PoA) outlines a variety of closely linked objectives designed to attain gender equality more generally, while one of its four areas of focus is gender, democracy, peace and conflict. Although these resolutions and the PoA are far-reaching in scope, to date their effectiveness is hindered by low implementation.

Since UNSCR 1325 was adopted in 2000 only 33 countries[1] have developed national action plans (NAPs) for its implementation, as called for by the Security Council in two Presidential Statements (United Nations 2004; 2005). Of the 54 members of the Commonwealth, only 5 countries have done so to date. Given that conflict has affected a number of Commonwealth countries, with numerous negative impacts on women and girls, there is a strong need for all member states to adopt and implement these resolutions. This need is exacerbated by the continued minimal presence of women in conflict resolution and peace-building processes in general.

The Commonwealth Secretariat is committed to assisting its members to develop NAPs to implement UNSCR 1325 and the PoA in light of the urgency of the situation. The purpose of this book is to contribute to these efforts. Chapter 2 outlines theories on the role of women in conflict, peacemaking and post-conflict reconciliation to contextualise the discussion and also provides more information on UNSCR 1325 (which is supplied in full in the Annex). Chapter 3 presents a number of case studies of countries undergoing and/or recovering from conflict where, despite their extensive engagement in work for peace and other activities to bring an end to violence, women have not been included in formal peace-building and conflict resolution processes. It also offers a number of reasons for why this has been the case.

Chapter 4 then examines countries in which women's engagement in conflict resolution has led to the adoption of NAPs. A central question considered here is what practices or linkages contributed to the achievement of greater numbers of women in decision-making organs generally or in peace-building more specifically. However, it is important to note that the adoption of a NAP does not necessarily mean that women were involved in formal processes of conflict resolution and/or the signing of peace agreements. Thus this chapter also examines whether – and, if so, how – NAPS have contributed to strengthening women's engagement in conflict resolution, peace-building and overall political participation. The final section of the chapter examines the two examples in the Commonwealth of countries that have implemented NAPs although not experiencing conflict domestically.

Chapter 5 then uses paragraphs from UNSCR 1325 to trace the progress selected Commonwealth countries have made in attaining the goals outlined therein. Some possible scenarios are also suggested concerning the future prospects for women's political participation in these countries.

Finally, in light of the examined impact of NAPs on women's participation in peace processes in particular and political participation more generally, Chapter 6 frames some recommendations for the Commonwealth Secretariat, strategic partners and member states.

This publication is informed by a desk review of relevant research that examines the role of women in conflict prevention, resolution and peace-building in general. The assessments made are based on the author's interpretation and analysis of this research.

Note

1. As of November 2011, according to the NGO PeaceWomen. More information, including links to the existing plans, can be found at: www.peacewomen.org/pages/about-1325/national-action-plans-naps

2. Women, Conflict and UNSCR 1325

The role of women in conflict and post-conflict countries

While much of the literature on women in conflict situations traditionally focused on them in a narrow capacity as victims, recent research has uncovered the multidimensional impact of conflict on women. Although women are severely affected by war – vulnerable to sexual and gender-based violence including rape, forced conscription, sexual slavery, abduction and forced impregnation among other atrocities – they are not simply victims but can play more proactive roles as well (Moser & Clark 2001). On the one hand, women are sometimes advocates of violence, inciting men to fight as well as themselves playing principal roles in fighting (McKay 2005; Cohen 2009). On the other hand, they often also play instrumental roles in advocating for peace and maintaining community stability (Bennett et al. 1995; Sørensen 1998; NUPI & Fafo 2001; Anderlini 2007). Many women take on the role of household head and primary income earner for their families in the absence of their men folk and become responsible for ensuring the economic and social welfare of their families. In addition, women have become an effective part of peace-building initiatives, engaging in post-conflict reconstruction and reconciliation and being actively involved in peace processes in countries including Pakistan, Rwanda, Sierra Leone, South Africa, Sri Lanka and Uganda.

Good practices of women advocating for peace take a variety of forms. Among other activities women have met and spoken with rebels in an effort to get them to lay down their arms; they have organised and participated in mass protests on the streets; they have spoken out over the airwaves about peace; and, despite no formal invitation, they have attended meetings where conflict resolution efforts were underway. Through civil society alliances and NGOs women have been instrumental in trying to make sure that women's opinions and needs are placed on the national agenda, especially their desire for peace.

However, notwithstanding women's active roles in conflict resolution and peace-building they continue to remain largely marginalised from the formal processes of peacemaking, with their work often not receiving recognition in these channels (Boyd 1994). Many women, including fighters, are expected to return to domestic or traditional roles following conflict (Hale 2001) and are left out of peace-building processes that take place at the level of the state (Mugambe 1997).

Despite the 10-year existence of United Nations Security Council resolution (UNSCR) 1325 (discussed below), women's engagement in conflict resolution and peace-building has yet to be institutionalised and the recognition of the importance of including women in peace processes has not resulted for the most part in their increased visibility across all sectors. Women continue to face barriers that impede their full political participation and representation (Norville 2011). They remain underrepresented in peace talks, peace settlements and peacekeeping missions; post-conflict rehabilitation measures still fail to take women's needs into account, including disarmament, demobilisation and reintegration (DDR) processes and relief and general development interventions; and physical insecurity plagues women both during times of conflict as well as in the ostensible 'post-conflict' period when rates of rape and other forms of sexual and gender-based violence remain high.

A report from the United States Institute for Peace notes the following troubling statistics culled from various sources: 31 out of 39 cases of active conflicts were ones that recurred after peace settlements had been signed, and none of these recurrent conflicts had included women in the peace process; women represented fewer than 3 per cent of signatories to peace agreements; and of 11 peace negotiations, women's participation averaged less than 8 per cent (Norville 2011).

Some scholars have argued that the changing roles of women during conflict situations offer potential opportunities for transformation: greater responsibilities assumed during wartime will provide women with greater levels of confidence, which can potentially transform social relations and patterns as well as increase women's political participation, leading in turn to greater gender equality and sustained peace (UNIFEM 2006; Mzvondiwa 2007).

In contrast, other scholars have argued that the reality is that in many instances where women have played instrumental roles in bringing an end to conflict, such activism has failed to yield positive results in the post-conflict period (Nzomo 2000; El-Bushra 2003).

UNSCR 1325: In support of women in peace-building processes

UNSCR 1325 was passed unanimously on 31 October 2000. It was the first resolution ever passed by the Security Council to specifically address the impact of war on women and women's contributions to conflict resolution and sustainable peace.

The purpose of the resolution was to call attention to the various ways in which women are affected by conflict so that governments could adopt a gender perspective in post-conflict reconstruction. Also emphasised in the resolution is the need for governments to support women's participation at all stages of peace negotiation – from conflict prevention and management to conflict resolution – and ensure they are represented in key decision-making positions for peace negotiations. Consequently, among its components the resolution calls for the recognition of the diverse ways in which conflict affects women so that interventions can better address their needs. This includes gender mainstreaming in peacekeeping operations and taking steps to ensure that women are full participants in peace processes, with the belief that such involvement could potentially enhance international peace and security. The resolution's four pillars are prevention, protection, participation and relief and recovery.

In addition to 1325, the UNSC has passed resolutions 1820 (2008), 1888 and 1889 (2009) and 1960 (2010), all geared to addressing women in conflict. They identify sexual violence as a security issue warranting the intervention of the Security Council and introduce measures aimed at addressing the issue, including the creation of the Office of a Special Representative of the Secretary-General on Sexual Violence in Conflict. A plan to monitor countries' progress in implementing 1325 was adopted by the UN in October 2010.

The development and implementation of national action plans (NAPs) is one of the key ways through which governments take concrete steps to implement 1325 in their respective countries. The plans spell out the actual activities that governments will undertake to translate 1325 into policies and objectives at the domestic level. However, as mentioned in Chapter 1, very few countries in the Commonwealth have implemented NAPs; of the five that have done so, only three are countries that can be classified as post-conflict.

3. Women's Peace-building Efforts across the Commonwealth

There is clear evidence of women's active local-level engagement in promoting peace, and yet as previously noted this often does not translate into involvement in higher-level peace-building processes. This exclusion can have adverse implications for the protection of women in these societies as well as impede long-term resolution of the conflicts.

Overall, the countries of the Commonwealth have seen a relative decline in the number of conflicts in the 2000s relative to the previous decade. During the 1990s at least 10 Commonwealth countries were engaged in full-scale conflict – including Mozambique, Papua New Guinea, Rwanda, Sierra Leone and Uganda – with peace agreements reached in most by the early years of the twenty-first century. Women played instrumental roles in many of the efforts to bring these conflicts to an end. Yet, in a large number of countries women's substantial efforts were not recognised in formal negotiations and their perspectives and insights were not included in the final peace agreements or in post-conflict reconciliation efforts.

The case studies in this chapter show where women's activism during conflict has not led to significant progress on women's rights. Also proffered are reasons as to why activism has failed to yield positive results.

Examples of limited engagement in peace negotiations

This section reviews the cases of Sierra Leone, Mozambique, Zimbabwe, Solomon Islands and Papua New Guinea (Bougainville) as illustrations of this problem.

Sierra Leone
Between 1991 and 2002 civil war raged in Sierra Leone with far-reaching destructive impacts on the lives of women and girls. Atrocities committed included rape, mutilation and forced enslavement. Some women and girls were coerced into 'marriages' with rebels while others were forcefully conscripted or used as porters and required to carry rebel equipment and supplies for miles. However, women in Sierra Leone were

more than victims. Not only were there recorded cases of willing female combatants (Coulter 2008), but women were also active in other arenas as well. Many became primary breadwinners as men were involved in the war effort, and they were also instrumental in organising for an end to the conflict.

Despite relatively high levels of marginalisation of women from political structures at both the formal and customary levels, stemming from cultural barriers under-pinning a primarily patriarchal society, women nevertheless were able to play instru-mental roles in advocating for the end of violence and building peace. Through civil society organisations such as the Sierra Leone Women's Forum and the Sierra Leone Women's Movement for Peace (SLWMP) women mobilised against war by, for example, organising protests, marches and demonstrations calling for peace; attending forums such as the UN Fourth World Conference on Women (held in Beijing in 1995) to bring the war to international attention; advocating for and playing instrumental roles in two national consultations that successfully called for elections before peace; and promoting women's political participation during the 1996 election campaigns (Jusu-Sheriff 2000; Pham 2004; Ogunsanya 2007; Castillejo 2009).

Such engagement yielded some positive dividends. Although at first women were not part of any of the formal dialogue concerning peace and were excluded from the main peace negotiations of Abidjan in 1996 and Conakry in 1997, at least two female representatives were included in the peace talks held in Lomé in 1999 and the resulting Peace Agreement mentions the importance of paying attention to women's special needs in the post-conflict context (Ogunsanya 2007; Barnes 2010).

Women led efforts of concerted bargaining for inclusion, including sit-ins and marches in front of parliament as well as lobbying key regional organisations involved in peace-building operations. Women's civil society organisations monitored government activities and also contributed to strengthening capacity building for women through the provision of gender-sensitive training at all levels of government including for parliamentarians, the judiciary and the media (Ogunsanya 2007).

However, some activists such as Yasmin Jusu Sheriff (2000) believe that the movement did not translate into greater participation of women in formal peace-building processes due to a combination of the unwillingness of male politicians to disturb the status quo and the reticence of women themselves. For the most part women went back into the private sphere once peace was declared. Levels of sexual and gender-based violence remain high in the aftermath of conflict, with little punitive action taken. The Family Support Unit (a post-war creation within the police responsible for investigating domestic and sexual violence against women) noted that out of 927 crimes reported in 2009, there were no convictions (Jean-Matthew 2010). Women remain underrepresented in governance (accounting for just 17 of 124 members of parliament) and women's groups have been unsuccessful in instituting a 30 per cent quota for parliamentarians.

Such findings are reinforced by those of Barnes (2010), who found that formal insti-tutional mechanisms did little to include women in the peace process. For example, the United Nations Mission in Sierra Leone (UNAMSIL) failed to incorporate a gender mandate in its mission, only briefly referring to women. Steps taken to address the role of women appear to be afterthoughts and were poorly funded, with negative implications for women in the demobilisation process as well as in some types of humanitarian assistance.

Barnes also points to the importance of context-based interpretations of 1325; the absence of domestic actors in the development and implementation of the mandate of UNAMSIL meant there was little consideration of specific ways in which to incorporate local understandings of gender equality or to bring about change (ibid.). What measures were adopted were limited by cultural barriers, and more emphasis needed to be paid to addressing these as well as other underlying attitudes, structures and practices that prevent the achievement of goals to promote women's involvement. Furthermore, it is not enough to simply advocate for women's political participation; also needed is an emphasis on education and training so that women can be effective in these positions. Sustained efforts to address women's lack of economic and social rights, which contribute to women's general marginalisation, are instrumental as well.

Despite these limitations, one could argue that women's activism has paved the way for some changes, at least at the institutional level, to help improve women's rights and standing in Sierra Leone society. They also contributed to the development of the country's National Action Plan (discussed in Chapter 4).

In line with recommendations made in the 2004 report by the Truth and Reconciliation Commission (TRC), which called for the repeal of discriminatory statutory and customary laws and the reduction of sexual and gender-based violence against women, the Government passed three 'Gender Bills' into law in 2007: the Domestic Violence Act, the Registration of Customary Marriage and Divorce Act and the Devolution of Estates Act. These Acts address three key areas: greater protection of women from domestic violence, women's inheritance rights, and regulations pertaining to early marriage and divorce.

Although women were not included for the most part in formal peace-building mechanisms during negotiations leading to the end of conflict, the passage of laws aimed at improving their lives as well as the development of the NAP in 2010 – with its focus on mechanisms to prevent conflict, prosecute and punish perpetrators as well as boost women's political participation – are all positive steps. The tangible outcome of these interventions remains to be seen, but the inclusion of monitoring and evaluation mechanisms within the plan means that such assessments should be forthcoming.

Mozambique

Women have a long history of involvement in conflict in Mozambique, first playing instrumental roles in the Liberation Front of Mozambique (FRELIMO) as part of the national liberation movement (1964-1974) and then during the civil war (1976-1992). They were active in a multitude of contexts including as breadwinners, fighters and advocates for peace. However, despite the apparent visibility of women in these different areas, some authors have pointed out that the prevailing cultural attitudes still either dictated or constrained what women accomplished. For example,

Chingono (1996) found that activities encouraged within the women's wing of FRELIMO included sewing, cooking and dancing and simply served to reinforce women's traditional roles and activities.

In the aftermath of war it appeared that women had made some gains. For example, in the 1994 elections – the first to be held after peace was established – women gained 30 per cent of the seats, second only to Rwanda. Political institutional rules also favoured women thanks to a quota system adopted by FRELIMO, as one third of party candidate lists must be allocated to women. Despite these apparent successes, however, the argument holds that institutional changes that accord political, social and economic rights to women can have limited practical success if there are cultural barriers. For the most part, women were not involved in the reconstruction processes and in many cases they simply reassumed their traditional roles (Barron 1996). Thus, despite their participation in conflict and conflict resolution, many Mozambican women remain subject to patriarchal family authorities and male community leaders who have paid little attention to the new roles women adopted during the conflict (Mzvondiwa 2007).

In addition, the absence of comprehensive gender analysis – or the existence of an analysis that considered women in limited ways, such as simply victims – resulted in the implementation of policies and programmes that did not effectively address their needs. This included demobilisation programmes that failed to recognise that some 'wives' of ex-combatants might have been forced into marriage and so should be given the option of resettlement with their families rather than having to accompany demobilised soldiers who received DDR packages (Jacobson 1999).

Zimbabwe

Zimbabwe presents another example of the marginalisation of women following involvement in liberation struggles. Again, despite the rhetoric of empowerment of women as part of a broader social justice agenda, it would appear that on achieving independence, such appeals and concerns took a backseat and men were primarily responsible for decision-making and crafting the new regime. Several reasons have been put forward to explain this, including the prevalence of men who fail to acknowledge women's equality (Nzomo 2000).

Solomon Islands

There are similar findings from Solomon Islands, where despite women's key activities in promoting peace during ethnic tensions between 1998 and 2000, culturally rooted beliefs about the respective roles of women and men did not allow women to play a major role in the aftermath of conflict (Webber & Johnson 2008). Thus, despite women's instrumental roles in lobbying for peace, formal negotiations left women out (Charlesworth 2008).

Papua New Guinea (Bougainville)

Bougainville in Papua New Guinea offers a somewhat different perspective regarding the role of culture. Central to women's successful engagement there was their ability to couch their work within the broader idea of motherhood, which had a special local resonance due to the matrilineal tradition in which land, culture and knowledge are inherited through the female line (Saovana-Spriggs 2007, cited in Charlesworth 2008).

Women were very much engaged in peace-building efforts, including peace negotiations at all levels (ibid.). Women's groups such as the Letina Nehan Women's Organisation (LNWDA) and the Bougainville Inter-Church Women's Forum (BICWF) organised a range of activities to promote peace and conflict resolution as well as general development. Even during the most intense violence in the early 1990s, women launched peace activities at village level, including going into the bush to talk to young fighters and try to persuade them to return to their homes (Howley 2002). Later, women organised peace demonstrations, conferences and meetings. Women's church groups were the vehicles for meetings between women from different areas of the island with different allegiances in the conflict. The Bougainville Inter-Church Women's Forum, held over a week in August 1996 in Arawa, became a turning point in the conflict, with 700 women attending from all parts of the territory.

However, even within a cultural context that supported women, Charlesworth (2008) still found that public life was for the most part closed to women; out of 40 members of government, only 3 are women.

Why women's engagement may be limited following conflict

The above examples show that, in many cases, women's active involvement in various components of conflict and peace do not translate into greater roles for them in formal avenues of peacemaking or political representation. A number of reasons have been advanced to explain this, including the failure of subsequent policies to question gender roles; the prevalence of cultural barriers that impede women's greater involvement; the absence of sustained promotion of gender equality at both the international level and the level of the state; structural constraints on women's time; and differences among women on the objectives and central concerns following conflict.

Regarding the first point on the ascription of gender roles, and despite a plethora of research that has uncovered the various ways in which war affects women, responses to women in the aftermath of conflict still seem to locate them in one category: as victims. Thus interventions, from state-instituted processes to relief projects, put in place policies and projects that neglect the multiplicity of women's experiences and can even reinforce traditional gender roles. This has implications for a host of reintegration efforts including security sector reform, reform of the judiciary and law, and DDR.

Even when women are considered as agents, it is still in a very narrow capacity – for example, as peace-builders who are intrinsically wired toward more co-operative and collaborative behaviour because they are women. This can negatively affect DDR processes, which historically have failed to be gender sensitive (UNIFEM 2004). By ignoring women's roles as combatants, DDR activities disempower women who are not deemed eligible to participate in the reintegration packages received by combatants.

Neglecting the impact of stigma on self-esteem and confidence can also rob women of valuable means to rebuild their lives (M'Cormack-Hale 2009). In addition, reintegration programmes often fail to take into account women's views; this is especially problematic since women are affected by mechanisms set up for ex-combatants to reconcile and return to their communities (Norville 2011).

One-dimensional perspectives of women can also have implications for their political participation. Part of this problem paradoxically stems from the reasons given to explain and support the need to include women in peace-building efforts. One branch of thinking lodges women's instrumental roles in conflict resolution in attitudes that ascribe certain qualities to women: that as mothers, nurturers and so on they are more likely to be consensus-builders and better negotiators.[1] On this basis, women are seen as inherently more peaceful than men. However, as a number of scholars have pointed out, such a perspective can in turn limit women's inclusion in formal peace-building efforts (Barnes 2010) as they are expected to return to what are assumed to be their foremost concerns – home and family – at the conclusion of conflict. As Dianne Otto has written: 'If women are admitted on the understanding that their special contribution arises from their womanly instincts, it follows that their political agency will be limited to what is made possible by that representation and restricted to "feminised" tasks involving nurturing and mothering' (2006, cited in Charlesworth 2008: 350). From this perspective, the expectation that women should not be involved in formal peace-building operations is unsurprising.

There needs to be greater questioning of both masculine and feminine identities and/or roles and of what it means to be a woman or a man. Essentialised understandings of these variable categories – using biology or physiology to explain human social behaviour – can lead to rigidity that does not allow for sustained social transformations to occur but simply replicates old social patterns that continue to marginalise women.

Furthermore, positive advances in women's rights can only be effected with commitment to changes that encompass all sectors of society. As Nzomo writes, 'post-conflict reconstruction and attainment of sustainable peace entail the rebuilding of the social, economic, and political infrastructure and strengthening governance institutions to make them conducive to and supportive of economic and social development on a just and equitable basis, regardless of gender, ethnic, religious, cultural, racial and other social identities within society' (2000: 4). Thus, it is not enough to simply work toward increasing women's political representation or involvement in peace-building; ways must also be found to increase women's access to and participation in all segments of the society, including economic, political and social structures.

For this to occur, interventions must question the broader structures that underpin women's lack of engagement and involvement following conflict. Consequently, social relations are key. An understanding of the gendered power relations that exist at the community level must be interrogated and addressed rather than simply targeting women and/or men in isolation from the larger context (Bryne with Baden 1995).

At present even relief efforts are susceptible to treating women in a one-dimensional fashion. Humanitarian interventions in a variety of country contexts have been criticised for implementing projects where a focus on 'women's needs' can simply serve to reinforce traditional gender roles as well as contribute to the implementation of projects that are unresponsive to local demands (Baden 1997; M'Cormack-Hale 2009). The proliferation of training in activities such as cooking, hairdressing and sewing does little to transform gender relations and can create an excess of skills that lack a market.

In addition to widely prevalent social norms that locate their primary roles within the private rather than the public sphere, women also face structural constraints that impede their ability to be active in the political sphere. For example, a number of scholars have pointed out that women's time is constrained (see, for example, those cited in Mi-Hye 2006). Their responsibility for the economic and social welfare of their families, and drains on their time such as farm work, cooking and cleaning, do not leave women with much time for more politically oriented activities. Moreover, numbers are not enough – while quotas can ensure women's representation, they might not necessarily translate into effectiveness, which also needs attention paid to capacity building and training of women leaders.

The ad hoc adherence to and implementation of UN resolutions by the international community is another limitation. Even the UN, including the Security Council itself, is not immune. Gender mainstreaming within the UN is only spottily applied and women occupy just a few senior positions. Funding constraints of peacekeeping missions are another problem, and gendered initiatives are often not a priority (Binder et al. 2008).

An analysis was undertaken to commemorate the 10-year anniversary of UNSCR 1325 that aimed, through measuring how gendered UNSCR resolutions have been across the past 10 years, to identify the extent of internalisation by the Security Council of its own resolution. One of its findings was that the Council's country-specific resolutions often did not go far enough in incorporating the ideas or the language of 1325 (Butler et al. 2010). This finding is crucial given that instructions at the highest levels of international security play an instrumental role in guiding implementation on the ground (Barnes 2010) and set the example that gender concerns should be taken seriously at all levels.

Thus, the guidelines for peace support operations must in themselves be gendered as this not only reinforces the point that gender mainstreaming should be implemented at all levels, including the highest levels of international security, but can also direct how women are included in practice. They can guide the mandate of institutions on the ground, and even the makeup of the operation, to ensure that women play central roles and that analysis and activities are fully gendered. For example, because women's work often takes place at the local level or in the informal sphere, it is often still neglected by the international community despite the existence of resolutions that urge the contrary. This point is further underscored by Binder et al. (2008), who note that the lack of consistent implementation as well as language inclusion by the UN of the articles of 1325 is a significant barrier to its impact. They point also to the need for 'farther reaching gender-mainstreaming policies within the UN' (ibid.: 34) and touch specifically on how these limitations have affected women's participation in the peace-building process, one of the central concerns that underlie many of the case studies above.

Language that stresses the importance of engaging with *all* peacemaking efforts on the ground could be one step toward addressing this. Furthermore, even international peacekeeping efforts fail to put adequate emphasis on placing women in leadership positions, as the example of UNAMSIL illustrates (Barnes 2010). Thus, although the UN pays lip service to the need to incorporate women in key positions, it has failed to follow through on this. According to Anderlini (2007) there were no women among the 18 special representatives in conflict areas in the year she was writing, while a UN Security Council report indicates the number of women peacekeepers is very small – just 3 per cent of overall military contingents in 2010 (United Nations 2010).

Not only has the UNSC failed to consistently mainstream 1325 in its peacekeeping missions, but also specific country mandates and resolutions do not always address women's issues and concerns or refer to gender (Binder et al. 2008). Moreover, some peacekeeping missions do not have any personnel at all with experience on gender issues. This underlines the need for engagement at all levels, with countries that contribute troops advocating for women even among the highest levels of delegations responsible for peace-building and conflict resolution.

This is not to say that advances have not been made. As the 10-year analysis mentioned above points out, the inclusion of gender-sensitive language has increased, with over 80 per cent of the resolutions monitored by PeaceWomen referencing women in 2009 as compared to less than 5 per cent between 1998 and 2000 (Butler et al. 2010). The importance of language is highlighted in the positive impacts that have resulted in the field. As they note:

> 'The incorporation of language on sexual exploitation and abuse (SEA) has been important in mandates such as Darfur (UNAMID [African Union/United Nations Hybrid Mission in Darfur]) where Darfur's Gender Advisory Unit is one of the core substantive units and actively undertakes trainings, capacity-building, and technical assistance on gender mainstreaming, and specifically SEA. The peacekeeping mission in Timor-Leste (UNMIT [UN Integrated Mission in Timor-Leste]) represents another interesting example. Due to the call for gender mainstreaming in UNMIT's mandate, we saw the subsequent incorporation of gender units from the inception of the mission. Relating to women's participation in the electoral process, language in Haiti's (MINUSTAH [UN Stabilization Mission in Haiti]) resolutions led to ground-level, "long-term training initiatives aimed at developing leadership skills of women throughout the country who wished to serve as candidates for office"[2].' (Ibid.)

Such success reinforces the importance of language and helps underscore the urgency of ensuring that advocacy is undertaken to capitalise on these advances. As Butler et al. note, the situation is improving: for the total period covered (November 2000 to August 2010), 40.3 per cent of resolutions referenced women and or/gender but the number has been steadily growing over the years, with an 87 per cent high noted in 2009 (ibid.).

There are also some examples of women in high-ranking positions within the UN. For example, women have held senior positions on ad hoc tribunals, including as prosecutors at both the International Criminal Tribunal for the former Yugoslavia (ICTY) and International Criminal Tribunal for Rwanda (ICTR) as well as one (of four) presidents at the ICTR (Binder et al. 2008).

The international community must also make concerted attempts to identify and document local women's efforts at building peace and include them in programmes and policies aimed at changing gender relations and strengthening women's roles in society (International Crisis Group 2006; Binder et al. 2008). Building on what has already been accomplished is an instrumental way to ensure the success of interventions.

Notes

1. See Helms 2003 for an excellent review of the literature that supports this thesis.
2. United Nations Department of Peacekeeping Operations/Department of Field Support-Department of Political Affairs 2007.

4. Women and National Action Plans (NAPs)

The discussion in Chapter 3 has painted a somewhat gloomy overall picture of the ability of women to translate increased activism during conflict into involvement in formal mechanisms of peace-building as well as political participation more broadly. However, as the Commonwealth Plan of Action for Gender Equality 2005–2015 (PoA) notes, there have been some concrete accomplishments:

> 'In response to the target set by the Fifth Meeting of Commonwealth Ministers Responsible for Women's Affairs (5WAMM), requiring that by 2005 at least 30 per cent of those in political and decision-making positions should be women, 12 Commonwealth countries had achieved women's representation in parliament of between 20 and 30 per cent by October 2003, with three (Mozambique, New Zealand and South Africa) consistently attaining the 30 per cent target. Since 1999, 24 countries have recorded an increase in female parliamentary representation, and there has been an appreciable rise in the number of female Ministers and Deputy Ministers.' (Commonwealth Secretariat 2005: 19)[1]

National action plans (NAPs) can help countries be accountable to the laudable ideals and vision laid out in UNSCR 1325. This chapter provides a review of countries that have implemented NAPs and explores the differences between implementing countries recovering from conflict and countries primarily engaged in peacekeeping activities overseas.

Women's involvement in the adoption of NAPs

As already mentioned, NAPs have been adopted in 5 of the 54 Commonwealth countries. These are Rwanda, Sierra Leone and Uganda in sub-Saharan Africa and Canada and the United Kingdom in the industrialised North.

Rwanda

Rwanda is often cited as a success story in terms of translating women's roles in peace-building into political representation following conflict. In so doing, it offers support to the thesis that conflict can provide women with new opportunities. Given that many men were killed during the genocide, the resulting demographic shift (around 70 per cent of the population were women when it was over) meant that women assumed roles traditionally ascribed to men such as heads of households as well as taking up occupations typically dominated by men such as mechanics and cab drivers (Mzvondiwa 2007).

Although women did play a role in carrying out the genocide, their participation was minimal with 2.3 per cent of genocide suspects being women (Powley 2003). However, Tutsi women were targeted during the conflict and suffered from rape, abduction and torture as well as death. Forming the government in the aftermath of genocide, the Rwandan Patriotic Front (RPF) prioritised women's inclusion in governance and peace-building. Thus the Rwandan case also illustrates the importance of a proactive government in ensuring that women retain the new spaces occupied during conflict.

The Rwandan Government made sure to formalise roles for women within political institutional structures. A total of 20 out of 80 seats were set aside for women, and there are posts throughout various levels of government charged with addressing women's concerns as well as providing training in gender awareness (Mzvondiwa 2007). Some of the reasons for emphasising women's inclusion in post-war governance structures stem from the same essentialist arguments outlined above, namely that women are more naturally oriented toward forgiveness and reconciliation, as well as the argument that since they were most affected by the violence, they would be most likely to want to work to overcome it (Powley 2003). Thus, Rwanda shows that essentialist-based arguments can nevertheless result in increased inclusion of women in political participation. Furthermore, some would argue that the critical mass of women is contributing to the passage of legislation that addresses women's concerns. Women have been able to successfully lobby for greater allocation of health-care spending, for example, as well as enact changes to land inheritance laws to be more favourable to women (Norville 2011).

In addition, Powley (2003) found that RPF exposure to Uganda's political system, which also prioritised women's inclusion through a quota system, helped to foster a similar sense of the importance of gender inclusion. This suggests that encouraging Commonwealth countries to adopt NAPs can have the beneficial effect of helping to institutionalise and normalise the perception that women should be included in political institutions.

However, while Rwanda has done well in ensuring women's political representation, with mechanisms in place even before the launching of the NAP for 1325 in May 2010, some commentators have noted that its record in involving women in peace negotiations has not been equally good. For example, women were not well represented in the Gacaca[2] court system and although the post-genocidal courts do allow for greater representation, women's influence remains comparatively low (Binder et al. 2008).

Sierra Leone

One of the key benefits of NAPs is that they can be developed within a country's specific historical, political and social context, as reflected in Sierra Leone's plan launched in March 2010. Spearheaded by the Ministry of Social Welfare, Gender and Children's Affairs, in close partnership with civil society organisations led primarily by women – the West Africa Network for Peacebuilding Sierra Leone (WANEP) and the Mano River Union Peace Network (MARWOPNET) – the development of the plan also involved a broad spectrum of stakeholders including other government line ministries, parliamentarians and UN agencies.

The NAP established five priority pillars:[3]

1. Contribute to reduced conflict including violence against women/children;
2. Protect and empower victims/vulnerable persons especially women and girls;
3. Prosecute perpetrators effectively and safeguard women's/girls' human rights to protection (during and post-conflict) as well as rehabilitation;
4. Contribute to the increased participation and representation of women;
5. Ensure effective co-ordination of the implementation process including resource mobilisation, monitoring and evaluation of and reporting on the NAP.

As such, it highlights key areas for intervention and evaluation. The collaboration of so many varied stakeholders and the extensive involvement of local and international partners can help provide a strong framework for awareness raising, capacity building and overall monitoring and evaluation of the impact of the NAP, but it will take time for the effects of the plan to be identified and assessed.

Uganda

Uganda has suffered a long history of violence that can be traced as far back as independence. The present conflict has lasted over 20 years, with the Lord's Resistance Army (LRA) under rebel leader Joseph Kony being particularly brutal and committing acts of unspeakable violence. Women and children have been especially affected, subject to abductions, widespread rape and murder. According to the United Nations Children's Fund (UNICEF) an estimated 7,500 girls have been abducted and more than 1,000 babies born in captivity (cited in International Crisis Group 2006). In 2005 the conflict took a new turn as the LRA moved into the Democratic Republic of the Congo, and it has contributed to further destabilisation and conflict there as well as in Sudan (Binder et al. 2008). The conflicts have also led to widespread displacement and refugee flows.

However, as has been seen in other situations of conflict highlighted above, women were not only victims but also played active roles. The absence of men meant that women stepped into positions traditionally held by men including combatants, bread-winners and household heads (ibid.). Additionally, women have played instrumental roles in trying to bring the conflict to an end and address some of its impacts. Women in the north have been involved in a range of activities geared toward promoting peace, including demonstrations against violence and facilitating reconciliation between community members and former LRA members. Women have also worked to address the needs of victims of violence through, for example, the creation of a reception centre where formerly abducted girls are offered counselling services and life skills (International Crisis Group 2006). Most of their activities have been at the community level with very few opportunities for involvement in national-level peace talks, to which they have not been invited. Nevertheless, women do attend such talks. For example, and despite not being accorded an official voice in the negotiations, women travelled from various locations in Uganda by bus, donkey and on foot to peace talks being held in Sudan in 2006 to articulate their demands for peace (Nieuwoudt 2006; Norville 2011).

Although a key negotiator in trying to bring an end to the conflict is a woman (and former government minister), she appears to be a rare exception. This marginalisation is despite the fact that Uganda has been recognised as having one of the strongest and best organised peace movements in the region, one that builds on largely self-funded local activists who receive training and support from a Kampala-based NGO, Isis Women's International Cross-Cultural Exchange (Isis-WICCE). These peace animators in turn train other women to identify and mediate in community-based conflicts (International Crisis Group 2006). What is lacking however, is support (both political and financial) from the Government as well as donors for such locally grounded initiatives as well as inclusion in broader peacemaking activities. Although Uganda released the 'Uganda Action Plan on UN Security Council Resolutions 1325 and 1820 and the Goma Declaration' in December 2008, such support is not yet apparent.

Uganda's NAP attempts to incorporate the provisions of the documents it cites and focuses on implementing a legal and policy framework to advance women, improve access to health facilities, increase the availability of psychosocial services as well as medical treatment for women survivors of sexual and gender-based violence, and ensure adequate budgetary allocations to implement all the resolutions. Even before releasing the NAP, Uganda also had a quota system in place to ensure women's political participation through the reservation of a seat in every district (30) for women candidates. As of July 2011, women constitute 34.9 per cent of the legislature (IPU 2011). However, a central concern is that much of the plan has yet to be implemented, and that while on paper women appear to be equal to men, in practice inequality remains. Women need training to be able to perform well in the positions they occupy and to make a difference. Women are also still discriminated against – for example, while women are present within the military and serve alongside men, they face abuse and ill treatment (Kagumire 2010). Furthermore, despite their presence in the formal institutions of governance, much like in Rwanda they remain underrepresented in formal peace negotiations (Binder et al. 2008).

Women also continue to experience high levels of sexual and gender-based violence despite the existence of punitive laws and policies. This supports research showing that given the conditions of impunity that exist during periods of civil conflict, sexual violence can continue to rise even after official ceasefires (Norville 2011). However, having the policies on the books at least provides a framework through which abuses of the resolutions can be addressed and punitive measures pursued against perpetrators.

NAPs in countries at peace: a different experience

For countries at peace, NAPs appear primarily oriented toward the engagement of soldiers deployed with overseas local populations. A brief review of the NAPs in Canada and the United Kingdom illustrates these points. While the NAPs reveal commendable commitments, including increasing the numbers of women peacekeepers in overseas missions, there are constraints within countries that must first be addressed. Women tend to enlist in low numbers in the armed forces, which naturally has ramifications for the number of women that can be assigned to overseas posts. It is therefore important to provide incentives for such enlistment in developed countries that contribute troops to peacekeeping missions (Norville 2011). There is evidence that increasing women's participation as peacekeepers has a number of benefits including reduced rates of sexual abuse of civilians by troops (ibid.). Female peacekeepers can not only provide women with a greater sense of security but also, by serving as role models in the local community, help empower women to push for the right to participate in formal peace processes.

United Kingdom

The United Kingdom initially developed its NAP in 2006 but revised it in 2010, coinciding with the 10-year anniversary of 1325. In contrast to the previously mentioned Commonwealth countries, whose background of conflict resulted in plans with heavy domestic orientation, the UK plan has significant external emphasis, focusing especially on the country's work in conflict resolution and peace-building through deployment of peacekeeping troops. While the plan ensures that the four pillars of prevention, protection, participation and relief and recovery are covered, it principally provides guidelines for British engagement in the field (national and bilateral) and within multilateral institutions such as the UN and European Union (EU).

At the national level, elements of the plan include provisions for the training of British troops so that peacekeeping and peace-building operations are gendered. They also call for (an increase in) the inclusion of women in British military and police personnel deployed in peace support operations, as a step to making sure that women fully participate in any peace-building missions in which they are involved, and for political support of multilateral institutions. At the bilateral level the plan outlines actions being taken in specific field contexts, such as the Democratic Republic of the Congo, in support of 1325; at the multilateral level, it sets out a framework to support the overall strengthening of UN and EU measures in the implementation of 1325. The UK is currently reviewing its national action plan.

Canada

Canada's NAP was launched in October 2010 and shares many similarities with that of the United Kingdom in terms of a focus on overseas engagement since the country is also at peace domestically. The emphasis is on ensuring that personnel receive gender training so they can better understand and address issues related to women, peace and security in the field. It is also hoped that this will lead to interventions that emphasise the participation of women and girls in formal peace-building operations as well as ensure their equal access to development assistance. Moreover, the plan does not only cover the Canadian military; it also targets Canadian NGOs and recommends they adopt codes of conduct in their work to address issues of sexual exploitation and abuse in humanitarian crises.

Benefits of NAPS

Although the above has pointed to some of the constraints faced even by countries with NAPs, there are a number of benefits as well. One of the central tenets of 1325 is the inclusion of women at all decision-making levels including parliament and the judiciary. In many post-conflict countries, high numbers of women are reported in political positions. As already mentioned, Rwanda has the highest number of women parliamentary representatives worldwide. Women's representation has increased in other post-conflict countries as well. In Kosovo, women make up 28 per cent of parliamentary and municipal assemblies; 25 per cent of seats in the 2005 elections held in Afghanistan were reserved for women; and in the same year, women in Iraq gained 31 per cent of seats in parliament (UN Facts and Figures, cited in Binder et al. 2008).

While women's rights in these countries are still not fully guaranteed (for example, women including parliamentarians still face intimidation and abuse in Afghanistan[4]), numbers can nevertheless be important. Scholars have theorised that having a 'critical mass' of women represented politically – 30 per cent is widely recognised as the minimum necessary – makes a difference in terms of implementing gender-friendly laws and policies (Dahlerup 1988; Jaquette 1997; Sainsbury 2004). Along these lines, Powley (2006) found that women in the Rwandan Parliament have been able to advocate effectively to address problems faced by children and families, resulting in some gains at the level of policy outcomes.

Such gains are important since discriminatory national laws remain one of the primary barriers that constrain women's position in post-conflict societies. In sharing her experiences at a United States Institute of Peace conference on best practices for women's engagement in conflict, a female Ugandan Member of Parliament (MP) talked of being able to organise with other women MPs and advocate for gendered policies addressing women's needs in post-conflict reconstruction efforts. Among their successes were advocacy for trauma counselling, inclusion of maternity wards in the construction of planned hospitals and funding for women to start up their own businesses (Norville 2011).

The design of NAPs to facilitate implementation of 1325 can potentially contribute to the overall improvement of women's status in society since the resolution addresses a range of concerns that have served to undermine women's roles and adversely affect their well-being and empowerment.

While not necessarily resulting in women's engagement in formal peace processes, quota systems for women in politics are in place in at least two of the countries with NAPs (Rwanda and Uganda), reflecting the call in 1325 for increased political participation and representation of women. Women's political engagement can help to create conditions that encourage greater attention to their rights and roles once conflict has ended, and women can build on this momentum to encourage governments to adopt NAPS.

However, given that there are other countries where women were engaged in conflict resolution activities that have not translated into the creation of NAPs, the existence of such groups of women alone is clearly not enough. One thing the three post-conflict countries with NAPs have in common is political structures that are supportive, at least in theory, of women's rights; it appears then that both activism and supportive political structures are necessary to facilitate the adoption of NAPs. This calls for a committed government – one that recognises and appreciates women's efforts, believes that these efforts have been crucial for building peace and is willing to grant greater political representation to women through institutional mechanisms such as quotas to ensure that these efforts are successful. Greater political representation in turn can lead to changes in laws and policies that constrain women: for example, as mentioned above, women in Rwanda have actively campaigned for the revision of discriminatory laws as well as the implementation of other laws that promote women's socioeconomic development (Powley 2006).

In terms of countries at peace, the two examples looked at – Canada and the United Kingdom – are troop-contributing ones for which NAPs function as an effective way to guide conflict mediation activities in the field and ensure a gender perspective is part of all activities, from peacekeeping to peace-building. This in turn can help reinforce domestic mechanisms to improve women's involvement in peacekeeping processes and political participation more generally. Moreover, such countries can put political pressure on UN agencies and other multilateral institutions to implement 1325 at the highest levels and make sure they follow through on commitments, especially regarding the appointment of women in high-ranking positions within peacekeeping missions. This is especially important since humanitarian intervention often determines how resources are allocated following conflicts and where priority is placed. Ensuring that interventions at all levels are gendered – from peace-building mechanisms to humanitarian aid to development assistance – is a crucial step in reinforcing the message that women count. Moreover, where women are involved substantially in conflict resolution, peacemaking and peace-building processes, the likelihood of sustainable peace increases.

As the case studies illustrate, however, simply implementing NAPs is not the sole answer to the question of how to increase women's participation in peace-building processes and political representation and redress existing gender-based inequalities.

While NAPs are an instrumental component of holding countries accountable to 1325, a number of underlying factors need to be addressed that can hinder their effective implementation (or the adoption of NAPS in the first place). Women still face significant barriers in Rwanda and Uganda, for example, even though the governments are committed to ensuring their political representation. In both these countries, participation in peace-building processes remains low despite high numbers of women in government. The same is true of Sierra Leone, although there are fewer female parliamentary representatives there. Sexual and gender-based violence still require urgent attention and women continue to have limited educational and economic opportunities, to name just a few issues. While the value of a NAP is that it establishes precedents and sets in place legal structures that can reduce the constraints women face, as well as monitoring and evaluation mechanisms to keep track of the effectiveness of these instruments, underlying barriers that hinder effective implementation must also be dealt with.

Notes

1. Seven Commonwealth countries have over 30 per cent at the time of writing including Rwanda, which tops the table internationally at 56.3 per cent (IPU 2011).
2. The Gacaca courts are open-air community trials established in 2001 to help the Government expedite the huge numbers of prisoners accused of genocidal acts. They are based on traditional or grassroots systems of communal justice where judges come from the community and trials are public events. The courts operate alongside the ICTR and handle cases of defendants who, while not implicated in the planning of genocide, nevertheless participated in acts of killing. The public nature of the trials, as well as the involvement of victims in the sentencing of those found guilty, is also meant to promote national reconciliation and healing.
3. The full Sierra Leone National Action Plan can be accessed at: www.peacewomen.org/assets/file/NationalActionPlans/sierra_leone_nap.pdf
4. Sitara Achakzai, a female Afghan politician, was killed by the Taliban in 2009 (HuffPost 2009) and another prominent female politician, Malalai Joya, has received numerous threats against her life (BBC News 2005).

5. Peace and Conflict in the Commonwealth

The first part of this chapter uses paragraphs from UNSCR 1325 to chart the progress made by selected Commonwealth countries in attaining the goals outlined by the resolution. The extracts are in italics while the accompanying text provides examples of how the actions called for have been implemented in the various country contexts. The second part of the chapter offers some possible future scenarios regarding women, peace and conflict in the selected countries.

Implementation of UNSCR 1325 in selected countries (2000–2011)

India
Urges the Secretary-General to seek to expand the role and contribution of women in United Nations field-based operations, and especially among military observers, civilian police, human rights and humanitarian personnel

2010: Female Indian peacekeepers on the streets of Liberia have contributed to the involvement of women in Liberian society, particularly the police force. 'The numbers speak for themselves. Five years ago, one in 20 police personnel was a woman. Now, nearly one in five is female. According to UNMIL [the UN Mission in Liberia], applications from women to join the police force tripled the year after the female Indian peacekeepers arrived' (Ford & Morris 2010). This speaks interestingly to the role of women peacekeepers as members of states that are helping to implement UNSCR 1325 abroad while their own country sometimes struggles to meet its demands.

Nigeria
Urges Member States to ensure increased representation of women at all decision-making levels in national, regional and international institutions and mechanisms for the prevention, management, and resolution of conflict

2001: 'Women in all walks of life are realising that to be an integral part of the democracy, they need to organise and be more radical. Nigeria has 36 states and 747 local government chapters yet ... it has only four female senators, five Ministers in the Federal government and one female Deputy-Governor of a state (Lagos). President Obasanjo, when he came to power in May 1999, echoing the Beijing Platform for Action, promised that 30 per cent of the decision-making positions in his government would be reserved for women, sadly this is not yet a reality' (International Alert n.d.).

2007: The National Gender Policy called for 35 per cent representation of women at all levels of decision-making. Although more women have been appointed to cabinet positions, however, the electoral model of first past the post still limits the participation of women in senatorial, parliamentary and local government elections. Women have to work very hard to gain political acceptance in a patriarchal society. 'Nigerian women feel especially aggrieved at their lack of political empowerment and their voices are among the loudest calling for a referendum on the Constitution' (International Alert n.d.).

Further urges the Secretary-General to seek to expand the role and contribution of women in United Nations field-based operations, and especially among military observers, civilian police, human rights and humanitarian personnel

2006: Nigeria took the lead among UN member states by providing about 49 women police officers to peacekeeping missions by the end of 2006. It pledged a similar police contingent to support the African Union mission in Darfur, Sudan in 2007 (Deen 2007).

Papua New Guinea (Bougainville)

Urges Member States to ensure increased representation of women at all decision-making levels in national, regional and international institutions and mechanisms for the prevention, management, and resolution of conflict

2001: 'In two agreements in Bougainville-Papua New Guinea... the only mention of women was as signatories of the peace agreement itself' (Bell & O'Rourke 2010: 941–80).

2005: 'Bougainvillean women have not attained the public power that they would like. For example, women argued for 12 reserved seats in the new Constitution of an Autonomous Bougainville, but achieved only three' (Saovana-Spriggs 2007: 106). 'It is striking that since the 2005 election, there are only three women members of the government, out of a total of 40' (Charlesworth 2008: 347–361).

Rwanda

Urges Member States to ensure increased representation of women at all decision-making levels in national, regional and international institutions and mechanisms for the prevention, management, and resolution of conflict

2001: Rwanda employed a three-ballot system in the March 2001 sectoral and district elections that effectively increased women's political participation (as well as youth participation). Voters were provided with three ballots: a general one, a woman ballot and a youth ballot. This effectively guaranteed that women would be able to get into office, thus fulfilling President Kagame's notion of 'partnership' (Powley 2003; Mzvondiwa 2007).

2003: 'The role of women was formalised in the constitution, which set aside 20 of the 80 seats in the Chamber of Deputies for women. Throughout all levels of government in Rwanda, positions have been created to address women's issues and gender concerns. At national level, the Ministry of Gender and Women in Development co-ordinates with the government in gender-mainstreaming policies, creating gender focal points in other key ministries and conducting gender awareness training. At provincial level, there are civil servants with gender and women portfolios. At district level, the post of vice-mayor for gender has been created and local women's councils are active at cell levels' (Mzvondiwa 2007: 103).

'Another mechanism used by the government is a parallel system of women's councils and women-only elections. These are grassroots structures, elected at cell level by women only (and then through indirect election at each successive administrative level), which operate in parallel with the general local councils, and represent women's concerns (Izabiliza 2005). The role of the women's council is one of advocacy rather than policy implementation. Women are involved in skills training and awareness campaigns. They articulate women's views and concerns on education, health, and security to local authorities. This system has been effective in that it brought some women into the national parliament. It breaks the traditional bonds that have characterised male dominance and women's subordination in Rwanda. ... However, ... the participation of women is still in its infancy; a lot needs to be done to fulfil these initiatives. For example, the women who participate at grassroots level and in the councils are doing great work, but their involvement is often disparaged as "volunteer", charitable or social' (Mzvondiwa 2007: 104).

2005: 'As of 2005, Rwanda held the world's highest representation of women in parliament with 48.8 per cent' (Binder et al. 2008: 22–41).

2007: 'In Rwanda today, women hold nearly 49 per cent of the seats in the Lower House of Parliament. This is the greatest representation worldwide, according to a tally by the Geneva-based Inter-Parliamentary Union. In 2003 the union reported that Rwanda "had come the closest to reaching parity between men and women of any national parliament", replacing long-time champion Sweden (Enda 2003). This set-up has seen women's contributions to good governance. Women began serving in the executive, legislative and judiciary arms of government. This kind of high-level involvement is likely to have a great impact on how girl children perceive their role in Rwandan society' (Mzvondiwa 2007: 104).

2011: As already noted, women now hold 56.3 per cent of the seats.

Solomon Islands
Urges Member States to ensure increased representation of women at all decision-making levels in national, regional and international institutions and mechanisms for the prevention, management, and resolution of conflict

2000: 'From the early days of the conflict, women sought to capitalise on cultural images of women as peacemakers, forming a Women for Peace group to bring the warring parties together (Leslie 2002). Despite this, no women were included in peace talks held in Townsville in 2000. RAMSI [the Regional Assistance Mission to Solomon Islands] has done little to draw on women's experience in conflict resolution in the Solomons. Although women welcomed RAMSI's arrival and the immediate effect it had on curbing lawlessness in the capital, women leaders feel marginalised in the peace-building process' (Charlesworth 2008: 347–361).

'During the conflict, women's groups joined together to call for peace and democracy. They also played a more active role, crossing boundaries to talk and pray with the warring groups (Kabutaulaka 2002: 23). In May 2000, women, especially those in Honiara, formed women's peace groups and were later contacted by women around Guadalcanal who joined them in their peace work to resolve the crisis (ibid.). The conflict exposed introduced systems, intended to uphold the rule of law, as weak and irrelevant. International lobby groups, aid donors and foreign governments, desperate for legitimate, neutral groups to act as local entry points, paid increased attention to civil society and non-government organisations, including women's groups. For women in Solomon Islands, their role in peace-making assisted in dissolving some of the barriers to their involvement in public life. Given that societal values, particularly in rural areas, are essentially conservative and patriarchal, this is a quantum leap from the previous position' (Corrin 2008: 169–194).

2002: 'Solomon Islands finally became a State Party to the Convention [United Nations Convention on the Elimination of All Forms of Discrimination against Women 1979] on 6 May 2002, nearly 24 years after the pledge of equality was made in the Constitution. Since rustication of the Convention, no plan of action for strategies to implement it has been developed, as required by the Beijing Platform of Action. Nor has Solomon Islands submitted a report to the CEDAW Committee' (Corrin 2008: 169–194).

2004: The final draft of the new constitution provided more rights for women than the previous one, with women's equality constitutionally guaranteed as a 'fundamental right and freedom'. The constitution also provided women with rights to equal opportunities in political, economic and social activities, employment, education and health care as well as the right to represent the Solomons in international organisations (Corrin 2008).

2006: Despite constitutionally guaranteed equality and the contestation of 26 women for one of the 50 seats in parliament, no women were elected in the 2006 elections (Charlesworth 2008). Women are underrepresented in other high-ranking positions as well. Of nine magistracy appointments, only two have been women, and of 940 local court bench appointments, just one has been female. On the other hand, there has been an increase in the number of women lawyers, with women forming the Women in Law Association of Solomon Islands in 2006 (ibid.).

2007: The draft constitution from 2004 had still not become law and was being reviewed by a Constitutional Review Congress. The change of government in late 2007 meant its fate was uncertain (Corrin 2007). Despite the constitutional guarantee of equality, the law and politics in Solomon Islands have often accorded markedly different treatment to women and men in practice (Pulea 1985 cited in

Corrin 2008:169–194). Although there are areas of law where legal barriers have been removed, sex-based inequalities continue to persist in other parts of the decision-making process (ibid.).

Sri Lanka

Encourages all those involved in the planning for disarmament, demobilisation and reintegration to consider the different needs of female and male ex-combatants and to take into account the needs of their dependants

2007: Women were recruited into the Liberation Tigers of Tamil Eelam (LTTE) and regarded as fighters on par with men, while still expected to maintain certain traditional moral standards. However, after the conflict these women's agency did not lead to political power or respect, and in fact they have been expected to revert to traditional roles as wives and mothers within society.

'The expanded space for females attained in the context of armed conflict may therefore not automatically translate into tremendous post-conflict social changes ultimately beneficial to women. In fact, Alison (2004) notes that civil society is uncertain how to respond to female ex-combatants in times of peace. Some of the most negative aspects of women's reintegration into society post conflict entail a need to hide their past participation in war from the Sri Lankan governmental authorities' (Jordan & Denov 2007: 59).

Uganda

Urges Member States to ensure increased representation of women at all decision-making levels in national, regional and international institutions and mechanisms for the prevention, management, and resolution of conflict

Although women played instrumental roles in fighting for the end of conflict, in general their work has been marginalised in formal peace-building structures. 'Thus the peace-building involvement of Ugandan women tends to reflect their traditional roles as "background workers" and actors off the scene. They are rarely involved in officially recognised – or "forefront" – formal peace negotiations; rather, they participate in the informal processes around the official meetings' (Binder et al. 2008: 22–41).

2005: 'The principal peace negotiator in the major conflict between the government and the LRA is a woman, Betty Bigombe. She has been a key actor in the conflict-resolution process since 1994. As a northern Ugandan, a former government minister, and therefore a recognised and prominent political figure, Bigombe has been well prepared to mediate between the LRA and the Ugandan government. Under very difficult conditions, Bigombe has been encouraging the LRA and the Ugandan government to sign a ceasefire agreement. Her efforts have resulted in the resignation of a number of high-ranking LRA commanders who laid down their arms to support efforts for peace. In September 2005 Bigombe prepared a draft peace agreement that Museveni accepted as the start for substantive negotiations. Bigombe's efforts are supported by a growing number of women activists' (ibid.: 22–41).

2008: While women have been very active in NGOs and in peace-building activities, they lack support from the government or the international community.

Yet, 'they need both political and financial support from key national actors and donors to have sustainable impact. This is where the problems start. Unfortunately, Ugandan women are in this respect in no better position than women in other African countries. Support is sparse, if it is given at all – despite Resolution 1325, which has the support of local women engaged in peace efforts on the ground' (ibid.: 22–41).

Afghanistan (a non-Commonwealth example)

Urges Member States to ensure increased representation of women at all decision-making levels in national, regional and international institutions and mechanisms for the prevention, management, and resolution of conflict

2003: 'The American government was initially discouraged by some experts from focusing on women in Afghanistan as it was feared this would alienate anti-Taliban forces whose support was required in the war against terrorism. But eventually women's issues were placed at the top of the agenda and the United States pressed for full participation of women at Bonn, the reconstruction conferences in Washington and Tokyo, and the Loya Jirga in Afghanistan. Media also played an extremely effective role in highlighting the Taliban's repression of women' (Council on Foreign Relations 2003). In this respect it should be noted that UNIFEM (2002) has indicated that overall levels of assistance to women in conflict are related strongly to media interest in the country's trauma.

'Currently, work is underway to ensure the mainstreaming of gender in various ministries and projects, and ensuring that the new constitution guarantees equal rights for women and men. Finally, the economic and physical security of Afghan women is inextricably linked to peace and security in the country as well as to its economic growth (Council on Foreign Relations 2003).

2005: 'Since the fall of the Taliban in Afghanistan, every government has included a minister of women's affairs; in Afghanistan's 2005 parliamentary elections 25 per cent of the seats were reserved for women' (Binder et al. 2008: 22–41).

Calls on all actors involved, when negotiating and implementing peace agreements, to adopt a gender perspective, including ... measures that ensure the protection of and respect for human rights of women and girls, particularly as they relate to the constitution, the electoral system, the police and the judiciary

While the Security Council's record in incorporating women's concerns has been inconsistent, its resolution on Afghanistan was one of only a few to contain specific mandates for the protection of women and children. Other countries include Burundi, Darfur, the Democratic Republic of the Congo and Timor Leste (Binder et al. 2008: 22–41).

2009: 'In response to widespread concerns about harmful traditional practices and endemic violence against women throughout Afghanistan, the Government enacted the EVAW law [Law on the Elimination of Violence against Women] in August 2009, which represents a significant legislative step towards ending harmful traditional practices. Civil society groups and the Ministry of Women's Affairs steered the law's development. Among its objectives, the law lists "fighting against customs, traditions and practices that cause violence against women contrary to the religion of Islam," and preventing and prosecuting violence against women' (UNAMA & OHCHR 2010: 3).

'Article 5 of the law lists 22 acts, the commission of which constitutes violence against women: rape; forced prostitution; publicising the identity of a victim in a damaging way; forcing a woman to commit self-immolation; causing injury or disability; beating; selling and buying women for the purpose of or under pretext of marriage; *baad* (retribution of a woman to settle a dispute); forced marriage; prohibiting the choice of a husband; marriage before the legal age; abuse, humiliation or intimidation; harassment or persecution; forced isolation; forced drug addiction; denial of inheritance rights; denying the right to education, work and access to health services; forced labour and marrying more than one wife without observing Article 86 of the Civil Code' (ibid.).

Possible scenarios for women, peace and conflict in these countries, 2011–2015

India

It is difficult to generalise with such a large country, particularly given the diversity of the conflicts in various areas. Overall, however, India appears to be moving toward greater inclusion of women in peace talks, creating initiatives for local women leaders and trying to address the concerns of each people as a whole, rather than simply dealing with the male leaders. There is a possibility that the next five years will bring some positive changes along the lines advocated by various aspects of UNSCR 1325. With the positive strides being made economically, India has the potential to improve rather than regress in the area of women's rights as more of the country becomes part of the global economy.

Nigeria

Women in Nigeria have made some progress over the past decade, but the majority of them have yet to be economically or politically empowered in any significant way. The major efforts at the moment centre around changing ingrained ideas regarding women in politics and capacity building on the ground to produce qualified women candidates for office. Progress in this area is possible but, barring some significant alteration in Nigerian policy, this will most likely take the form of incremental changes that will only add up to significant advances in the next decade or two (Muhammad 2010).

Papua New Guinea (Bougainville)

The push for women's involvement in government has stagnated since peace was achieved. Currently the only women elected are those mandated by the quota, so one possible way to bring about positive change would be to increase the quota.

Rwanda

Conditions for women will continue to improve in the country, largely due to the parity achieved in the Government and the emphasis on maintaining and growing the role of women in politics. The girls who are currently going to school will see the gender parity at high levels of government and, barring strong cultural influences to the contrary, this should perpetuate the acceptance of women in positions of authority.

Solomon Islands

Improvement for women will continue to be slow moving in this country. There has been much rhetoric about women's rights in the past 10 years but very little actual change. Unless measures are put in place to require a quota, women will very likely continue to be excluded from government and thus the decision-making processes in the country. There needs to be a commitment to the laws of equality already on the books and a push to implement further changes both in law and in actuality.

Sri Lanka

While women (at least on the Tamil side) were allowed and even encouraged to participate fully in the struggle, in the aftermath of the conflict their voices are being silenced and the role of women is barely acknowledged. Women have been told to return to their traditional roles in the home and few provisions have been made to include them in the peace process. Unless the leaders of the peace talks or the UN decide otherwise, there is a strong possibility that the lobbying of women's groups in Sri Lanka will go largely unheard and their needs unaddressed.

Uganda

Contingent on the existing grassroots and civil society organisations of women gaining traction in more official channels, the conditions for women will improve in Uganda. The fact that Uganda has a NAP on the books bodes well for the implementation of measures to include women in the peace process and other official government channels going forward.

Afghanistan (a non-Commonwealth example)

The next few years for women in Afghanistan will depend largely on whether the coalition forces currently in control of the country choose to focus solely on stabilisation or continue fledgling efforts to empower women under the ideals espoused by UNSCR 1325. Pure stabilisation (driven by a desire to get out as soon as possible) would likely sideline the rights of women in favour of putting a strong government in power and instituting a set of laws on the books that most of the (male portion of the) country will support. On the other hand, US Secretary of State Clinton has repeatedly committed the United States to improving the rights of women around the globe, so it appears likely that efforts to provide access to education and carve out a role in government for women will continue, as well as the creation of laws to protect women from harmful 'traditional' practices.

6. Recommendations

Recommendations for the Commonwealth Secretariat and other strategic partners

As noted above, the development of a NAP does not automatically translate into improvements in the socioeconomic and political welfare of women, and lack of implementation, action and accountability have been identified as the primary obstacles to concrete changes in women's lives (Butler et al. 2010). Thus a central role that the Commonwealth Secretariat and other strategic partners can play is to promote shared understandings of the purpose of NAPs as well as illustrate the problems faced and develop strategies to minimise them in newly implementing countries. Toward this end, the Secretariat can serve as a resource centre, documenting and sharing information on best practices through regular meetings with leadership across the Commonwealth. It can also help in the development of widely shared indicators and actions to address the central tenets of UNSCR 1325. The use of the same indicators across different countries would strengthen information collection and enhance comparability of data and measurement of progress in various contexts.

Address cultural beliefs

Chief among the obstacles noted are cultural beliefs (held by both women and men) that circumscribe women's roles. In many of the countries discussed earlier, following conflict men often expected women to retreat from the very public roles they might have played in advocating for peace and return to the home. In other cases, women themselves lacked confidence or also believed that their roles should be more private. Contextual implementation of NAPs is key to addressing some of these barriers. It would therefore be useful for the Secretariat and other international partners to identify key local partners and resource persons within each country who are familiar with its culture, can articulate some of the most serious constraints facing women and can brainstorm ways to address them. Such sessions can result in the creation of specific indicators as well as actions to effectively counter the barriers that culture can pose. Through the identification of areas of expertise, and drawing on the knowledge of female and male activists who have a history of working within the country and a familiarity with the specific issues, these barriers can be greatly minimised and even overcome. The participation of civil society will be crucial, and the Secretariat and Commonwealth Foundation can aid in the development of mechanisms to ensure civil society is included at all levels from programme planning to the development of indicators, programme implementation, feedback and modification.

Address structural inequalities: economic opportunities

While 1325 refers explicitly to the protection and empowerment of vulnerable persons, it does not outline all the various sources of this vulnerability. Where the Secretariat and other partners can be instrumental is in elucidating these specific vulnerabilities and in facilitating information sharing through the collation of constraints faced and best practices geared toward addressing these issues. For example, where women's vulnerability and lack of empowerment is rooted in comparatively few economic opportunities, one strategy could be to identify appropriate income-generating opportunities that enable women to be financially independent. This could include research directed toward finding new opportunities that transcend gender-specific roles such as sewing, cooking and so on. In countries recovering from conflict, war-affected women – including survivors of sexual and gender-based violence – need projects that can help them be financially sustainable and do not simply reinforce the status quo. Research into best practices as well as into potentially viable new income-generating activities for women can help spark ideas across countries and identify where and how to target limited resources while at the same time providing indicators that can be used to track progress.

Furthermore, given that some countries or regions have similar economies, the compilation and sharing of success stories on economic activities can be especially useful. Possible examples include the 'cows of peace' programme. This small-scale dairy programme – implemented by Heifer International Project in Byumba Province, Rwanda, with funding from the United States Agency for International Development (USAID) and the Ministry of Agriculture and Animal Resources – targeted both female and male beneficiaries and has contributed to significantly improving livelihoods and fostering reconciliation in this area of the country (Mutamba & Izabiliza 2005).

Address structural inequalities: laws

Resolution 1325 calls for special measures to protect women and girls from sexual and gender-based violence. The causes of violence against women are complex and multi-dimensional and necessitate an approach that focuses on a wide range of interventions. One area in which intervention is crucial is the law. A number of the case studies provide evidence that national laws can hinder the implementation of 1325; thus countries should be assisted in identifying contradictory laws and in designing new gendered ones that incorporate 1325 based on information-sharing and best practices across nations. This includes strengthening the legal environment to fully prosecute any and all abuses against women, be it during war or peace. Information about best practices in countries that have made sincere efforts to make domestic laws align with 1325 protocols, as well as examples of ways in which countries have changed these laws to conform with international standards as elucidated in 1325, should be shared.

Another area in which the law can be made to serve the interests of women's equality is through the enactment of policies oriented toward increasing women's political representation. Given that 1325 does not necessarily address the underlying barriers that impede women's access to decision-making positions, countries could be assisted to identify and address these issues. The examples of Rwanda and Uganda provide evidence that affirmative action policies have been an effective approach in bringing women into political positions. However, research has also shown that while numbers are important effectiveness is even more so (Ballington & Karam 2005; UNIFEM 2006). To this end, information should be collected and best practices shared of how countries have been able to increase both women's representation as well as their effectiveness while in parliament. Such discussions can aid in the development of indicators that will track not just numbers but also the ability of women leaders to put in place gender-friendly laws and policies that advance women's rights.

Address monitoring and evaluation

Many of the above points focus on ways to strengthen countries' implementation of NAPs since haphazard implementation can be almost as much a problem as lack of adoption. This should be a key focus area for the Secretariat, as should assisting member countries to develop NAPs. To this end, the Secretariat can work with partner countries to put in place incentives that encourage them to implement all aspects of the NAP. Monitoring and evaluation, often the weakest parts of project design, will be an important component of this. Through technical assistance, training and the collecting and sharing of information on how other countries are monitoring and evaluating their plans, the Secretariat can facilitate this process.

Another constraint that countries face is lack of resources. The Secretariat and other partners can provide the required technical and financial support to ensure countries can fulfil their commitments to the implementation of NAPs. Furthermore, tracking, publicising and sharing reports on countries' implementation progress could be one way to build accountability.

Develop a Commonwealth model for the adoption of NAPs

It is essential for the Secretariat to create greater visibility on the adoption and implementation of NAPs. This can be attained by creating a Commonwealth model through identifying priorities, exploring the benefits of adopting NAPs and emphasising their important contributions to the well-being of society. A major benefit, for example, is the establishment of a conflict resolution framework towards the promotion of peace at all levels of decision-making. The regular collection and dissemination of good practices in the development of NAPs throughout the Commonwealth will enhance their implementation. The Commonwealth Secretariat can develop appropriate guidelines on NAPs and hold regular trainings with member states to share these.

The Secretariat also needs to promote an intensive awareness-raising campaign in collaboration with strategic partners across member states, particularly in post-conflict countries and small states, to ensure that there is political commitment and that adequate human and financial resources are available for the full implementation of NAPs. Specific calendar events can be targeted to publicise NAPs and serve as a tool for peace-building and gender development. Moreover, the provision of financial and technical assistance to build human capacity in collaboration with strategic partners is pivotal to the plans' success.

Collaborate with other local and international actors

A host of organisations exist with the mandate of monitoring UN and country implementation of 1325 as well as encouraging countries to develop NAPs. While the unique niche of the Secretariat is its work with Commonwealth countries, it can nevertheless collaborate with these groups, sharing information, resources and best practices that have worked in different contexts. Some of these groups include the NGO Working Group on Women, Peace and Security (NGOWG),[1] which launched an initiative in 2009 geared toward providing UN policy-makers with information on the challenges of implementing 1325 commitments for women in conflict-affected societies. Another organisation, PeaceWoman,[2] has also worked on holding the Security Council accountable for implementing 1325 in its specific country resolutions and co-produced a handbook on this issue in 2010: 'Women, peace and security handbook: compilation and analysis of United Nations Security Council resolution language'. Various other civil society organisations and country groups (such as 'Friends of 1325') are active in awareness raising and promotion of 1325 and the adoption of NAPs. Discovering areas of collaboration and information sharing can be one way to maximise the Secretariat's efforts.

Support women's inclusion in peace processes

UNSCR 1325 calls for support of local peace initiatives, and yet this is one of the most under-served areas in terms of implementation. Given the evidence suggesting that women's engagement in conflict resolution is one component that helps facilitate the adoption of NAPs in countries currently experiencing or emerging from conflict, the Commonwealth Secretariat and other strategic partners can play a role in ensuring that national and international actors incorporate women's often locally based processes of conflict resolution. They can help to identify active women's organisations, provide assistance to enhance their conflict-resolution and peace-negotiating skills, and encourage states and relevant international actors to incorporate these women's groups in formal peace-building and conflict-resolution processes. In this way the Secretariat and other partners can play a central role in strengthening women's contribution and potentially increasing their well-being in the aftermath of conflict. They can also collect and share best practices in cases where countries' formal peace processes have incorporated and built on the advances made by local women's groups.

The involvement of women in formal peace-building mechanisms can also influence DDR processes. As noted earlier, these for the most part have not integrated a gender perspective and have thus often failed to incorporate women effectively or promote their well-being.

Work with countries at peace to prevent conflict and engender peacekeeping

Being at peace does not necessarily mean freedom from conflict as conflict can take several forms including barriers to women's access to resources, ethnic clashes, high levels of violence crime and the like. Moreover, given evidence that even when women are involved in peace-building efforts at the local or informal levels they fail to be incorporated into more formal efforts, the development of indicators on the protection of women and especially their inclusion in peace-building can serve as a surveillance mechanism to ensure countries have in place institutional structures that will facilitate women's involvement and integration should conflict occur. This is especially pressing in countries where internal unrest simmers and/or women face gendered forms of violence, such as domestic violence in the home or violence from drug trafficking – as is the case, for example, for some women in the Caribbean.

As already noted, the Secretariat can work with industrialised countries that are at peace to ensure that they build into their NAPs activities to support interventions such as ensuring more of those deployed go through training on gender sensitivity as well as increasing the overall numbers of women in the military through addressing domestic legislation that might impede women from enlisting in the first place.

Recommendations for Commonwealth member states

Document lessons learned and best practices

As mentioned earlier, only five Commonwealth countries have so far adopted NAPS. Ideally member countries yet to adopt NAPs should develop networks with these countries to learn and gain insights on good practices documented throughout the process. The lessons identified will serve as a good foundation to assist member countries towards the development and implementation of their own plans. Importantly, during the adoption of NAPs, new challenges and lessons identified should be documented and shared widely with relevant actors for future strategic intervention and the plans' implementation.

Take a multi-sectoral approach to the adoption of NAPs

Countries should involve all relevant agencies in the development of their NAP without restricting participation to gender-specific ministries. Relevant government agencies should include those responsible for meeting the Millennium Development Goals (MDGs), social development programmes, the public sector, internal affairs, foreign affairs and security services (defence, military and police). The process should be transparent and participatory at all levels of governance and across all sectors.

Collaborate with the private sector and civil society organisations

Beyond the government architecture, member states should involve and collaborate with the private sector and civil society at the national, regional and international levels related to the adoption and implementation of NAPs. The private sector and civil society play a critical role in sensitising the public and wider society. Standardised reporting guidelines should be made available to external actors and strategic partners, in an effort to promote their active participation and contribution towards the adoption and implementation of NAPs.

Align reporting of NAPs with the Commonwealth Gender Plan of Action

Member states should be urged to present reports on the status and implementation of NAPs at Women's Affairs Ministers Meetings (WAMMs). Such reports should be aligned with the Commonwealth PoA and harmonised with standardised reporting on the Beijing Platform for Action, CEDAW and UN Security Council Resolutions 1325, 1820, 1888, 1889 and 1960. This should be complemented by regular briefings aligned with regional peace and security policies through active co-operation with multilateral and regional organisations such as the Economic Community of West African States (ECOWAS), Southern African Development Community (SADC), African Union (AU), Organisation for Economic Co-operation and Development (OECD), European Union (EU) and UN.

Domesticate NAPs into national laws

Member states should consider the domestication of NAPs into national laws and relevant national policies and other planning frameworks such as poverty reduction strategies and national security, gender development and peace-building plans. National laws and regulations associated with 1325 and its follow-up resolutions should apply to private entities holding government contracts or receiving financial support to ensure the effective implementation of NAPs.

Dedicate funds for the implementation of NAPs

For successful adoption and implementation of NAPs, adequate resources are critical. There has been a call in this regard for a special fund similar to those that set aside resources for meeting the MDGs. There must be political will and commitment at the highest level of political leadership or else efforts to adopt and implement NAPs will not be easily realised. In Rwanda, for example, efforts for adoption of the NAP were centralised in the Presidency and all agencies were involved in its development and implementation. Furthermore, member states should call on institutions such as the UN and EU to support them with technical and financial resources towards developing NAPs.

Introduce accountability measures for NAPs

Monitoring and evaluation mechanisms including relevant indicators should be developed to effectively assess the implementation of NAPs with lines of accountability at all levels of decision-making. This can be achieved through periodic reporting to the legislature and to inter-state bodies regarding appropriate implementation, progress and results. With the support of international, regional and national organisations and institutions, member states can set up taskforces or equivalent structures to monitor, promote and evaluate the progress and results regarding the implementation of 1325 and its follow-up resolutions.

Notes

1. For more information on the organisation, see their website: www.womenpeacesecurity. org/about/
2. Information on PeaceWomen can be accessed at www.peacewomen.org/

References

Alison, M 2004, 'Women as agents of political violence: gendering security', Department of Politics and International Studies, University of Warwick, UK, cited in Ford & Morris 2010.

Anderlini, SM 2007, *Women building peace: what they do, why it matters*, Lynne Rienner Publishers, Boulder, CO.

Baden, S 1997, 'Post-conflict Mozambique: women's special situation, population issues and gender perspectives to be integrated into skills training and employment promotion', *BRIDGE Report* 44, June.

Ballington, J & Karam, AM 2005, *Women in parliament: beyond numbers*, revised edition, International Institute for Democracy and Electoral Assistance, Stockholm.

Barnes, K 2010, 'Lost in translation? UNAMSIL, Security Council resolution 1325 and women building peace in Sierra Leone', in F Olonisakin, K Barnes & E Ikpe (ed.), *Women, peace and security: translating policy into practice*, Routledge, London.

Barron, M 1996, 'When the soldiers came home: a gender analysis of the reintegration of demobilised soldiers, Mozambique 1994-96', University of East Anglia, Norwich.

BBC News 2005, 'Profile: Malalai Joya', 12 November, news.bbc.co.uk/2/hi/south_asia/4420832.stm (accessed 25 August 2011).

Bell, C & O'Rourke, C 2010, 'Peace agreements or pieces of paper? The impact of UNSC resolution 1325 on peace processes and their agreements', *International and Comparative Law Quarterly* 59(4): 941–80.

Bennett, O, Bexley, J & Warnock, K 1995, *Arms to fight, arms to protect: women speak out about conflict*, Panos Publications, London.

Binder, C, Lukas, K & Schweiger, R 2008. 'Empty words or real achievement? The impact of Security Council resolution 1325 on women in armed conflicts', *Radical History Review* 101: 22–41.

Boyd, R 1994, *Are we at the table? Women's involvement in the resolution of violent political conflicts*, Centre for Developing-Area Studies, McGill University, Montreal.

Butler, M, Mader, K & Kean, R 2010, *Women, peace and security handbook: compilation and analysis of United Nations Security Council resolution language 2000–2010*, PeaceWomen Project of the Women's International League for Peace and Freedom,

New York, www.peacewomen.org/assets/file/peacewomen_schandbook_2010.pdf (accessed 1 February 2011).

Byrne, B with Baden, S 1995, 'Gender, emergencies and humanitarian assistance', *BRIDGE Report* 33, November.

Castillejo, C 2009, 'Women's political participation and influence in Sierra Leone', *FRIDE Working Paper* 83, www.fride.org/publication/617/womens-political-partici-pation-and-influence-in-sierra-leone (accessed 23 September 2011).

Charlesworth, H 2008, 'Are women peaceful? Reflections on the role of women in peace-building', *Feminist Legal Studies* 16(3): 347–361.

Chingono, MF 1996, *The state, violence and development: the political economy of war in Mozambique*, Averbury, Aldershot.

Cohen, DK 2009, 'The role of female combatants in armed groups: women and wartime rape in Sierra Leone (1991–2002)', paper presented at the 50th annual meeting of the International Studies Association, New York, 15 February.

Commonwealth Secretariat 2005, 'Commonwealth plan of action for gender equality 2005–2015', Commonwealth Secretariat, London.

Corrin, J 2007, 'Breaking the mould: constitutional review in Solomon Islands', *Revue Juridique Polynesienne* 13(1): 143–168.

—— 2008, 'Ples bilong mere: law, gender and peace-building in Solomon Islands', *Feminist Legal Studies* 16(2): 169–94.

Coulter, C 2008, 'Female fighters in the Sierra Leone war: challenging the assumptions?' *Feminist Review* 88(1): 54–73.

Council on Foreign Relations 2003, 'The role of women in peacebuilding and recon-struction: lessons from Rwanda, East Timor, and Afghanistan', summary of a meeting held on 6 March, www.cfr.org/afghanistan/role-women-peacebuilding-reconstruc-tion-lessons-rwanda-east-timor-afghanistan/p5729 (accessed 22 September 2011).

Dahlerup, D 1988, 'From a small to a large minority: women in Scandinavian politics', *Scandinavian Political Studies* 11(4): 275–6.

Deen, T 2007, 'U.N. asks for more women peacekeepers', Inter Press Service (IPS), 16 March, ipsnews.net/news.asp?idnews=36958 (accessed 18 October 2011).

El-Bushra, J 2003, 'Fused in combat: gender relations and armed conflict', *Development in Practice* 13(2&3): 252–65.

Enda, J 2003, 'Women take lead in reconstruction of Rwanda', Women's eNews, www.womenenews.org/article/Rwanda.html, cited in Mzvondiwa 2007.

Ford, T & Morris, S 2010, 'India's female peacekeepers inspire Liberian girls', Inter Press Service (IPS), 24 October, www.ips.org/mdg3/indias-female-peacekeepers-inspire-liberian-girls-2/ (accessed 19 September 2011).

Hale, S 2001, 'Liberated, but not free: women in post-war Eritrea', in S Meintjes, A Pillay & M Turshen (ed.), *The aftermath: women in post-war transformation*, Zed Books, London.

Helms, E 2003, 'Women as agents of ethnic reconciliation? Women's NGOs and inter-national intervention in postwar Bosnia-Herzegovina', *Women's Studies International Forum* 26(1): 15–33.

Howley, P 2002, *Breaking spears and mending hearts: peacemakers and restorative justice in Bougainville*, Zed Books, London.

HuffPost 2009, 'Sitara Achakzai, female Afghan politician, gunned down by Taliban for women's rights work', 13 April, www.huffingtonpost.com/2009/04/13/sitara-achakzai-female-af_n_186168.html (accessed 25 August 2011).

International Alert n.d., 'Mapping report: Nigeria', www.badgerdesigns.com/alert/v1/pdfs/fin_niger.pdf (accessed 19 September 2011).

International Crisis Group 2006, 'Beyond victimhood: women's peacebuilding in Sudan, Congo and Uganda', *Africa Report* 112, 28 June, www.unhcr.org/refworld/pdfid/44c77a5b0.pdf (accessed 25 August 2011).

IPU (Inter-Parliamentary Union) 2011, 'Women in national parliaments: situation as of July 2011', www.ipu.org/wmn-e/arc/classif310711.htm (accessed 22 September 2011).

Izabiliza, J 2005, 'The role of women in''' reconstruction: experience of Rwanda', presentation delivered at Empowering Women in the Great Lakes Region: Violence, Peace, and Women's Leadership Conference, June www.unesco.org/new/fileadmin/MULTIMEDIA/HQ/SHS/pdf/Role-Women-Rwanda.pdf, cited [as Izibiliza 2003] in Mzvondiwa 2007.

Jacobson, R 1999, 'Complicating "complexity": integrating gender into the analysis of the Mozambican conflict, *Third World Quarterly* 20(1): 175–87.

Jaquette, JS 1997, 'Women in power: from tokenism to critical mass', *Foreign Policy* 108 (Fall): 23–37.

Jean-Matthew, T 2010, 'Sierra Leone: rape suspects have a field day, *Daily Nation*, 12 February.

Jordan, K & Denov, M 2007, 'Birds of freedom? Perspectives on female emancipation and Sri Lanka's Liberation Tigers of Tamil Eelam', *Journal of International Women's Studies* 9(1): 42–62.

Jusu-Sheriff, Y 2000, 'Sierra Leonean women and the peace process 2000', Conciliation Resources, www.c-r.org/our-work/accord/sierra-leone/women-peace.php (accessed 30 December 2010).

Kabutaulaka, TT 2002, 'Intervention and state-building in the Pacific: the legitimacy of "co-operative intervention"', cited in Corrin 2008.

Kagumire, R 2010, 'Women in the Ugandan military: no family planning services, no promotions', 8 November, www.voicehub.org/blog/women-uganda-military-no-family-planning-services-no-promotions (accessed 23 August 2011).

Leslie, H 2002, 'Gendering conflict and conflict management in the Solomon Islands', *Development Bulletin* 60: 13–16, cited in Charlesworth 2008.

M'Cormack-Hale, F 2009, 'NGOs and women's capabilities in post-war settings: the case of Sierra Leone', *JENdA: A Journal of Culture and African Women Studies* 15: 76–105.

McKay, S 2005, 'Girls as "weapons of terror" in Northern Uganda and Sierra Leonean rebel fighting forces', *Studies in Conflict and Terrorism* 28(5): 385–97.

Mi-Hye, C 2006, 'Gender, leisure and time constraint: employed men and women's experiences', *Development and Society* 35(1): 83–105.

Moser, CON & Clark, FC 2001, *Victims, perpetrators or actors? Gender, armed conflict and political violence*, Zed Books, London.

Mugambe, B 1997, 'Women's roles in armed conflict and their marginalization in the governance of post-conflict society: the case of "Luwero Triangle"', Eighth OSSREA Competition on Gender Issues, Organisation for Social Science Research in Eastern and Southern Africa, Addis Ababa.

Muhammad, M 2010, 'Nigeria: in the shadows of men – women's political marginalisation', allAfrica.com, 12 March, allafrica.com/stories/201003130001.html (accessed 7 October 2010).

Mutamba, J & Izabiliza, J 2005, *The role of women in reconciliation and peace building in Rwanda: ten years after genocide*, National Unity and Reconciliation Commission (NURC), Government of Rwanda, Kigali.

Mzvondiwa, CN 2007, 'The role of women in the reconstruction and building of peace in Rwanda: peace prospects for the Great Lakes Region', *African Security Review* 16(1): 99–106, www.iss.co.za/uploads/ASR16_1NTOMBIZODWA.PDF (accessed 8 December 2010).

Nieuwoudt, S 2006, 'Ugandan women march for peace talks', International Relations and Security Network, 30 November, www.isn.ethz.ch/isn/Current-Affairs/Security-Watch-Archive/Detail/?ots591=4888caa0-b3db-1461-98b9-e20e7b9c13d4&lng=en&id=51789 (accessed 6 December 2010).

Norville, V 2011, 'The role of women in global security', *Special Report 264*, United States Institute of Peace, Washington, DC, January, www.usip.org/files/resources/SR264-The_role_of_Women_in_Global_Security.pdf (accessed 24 August 2011).

NUPI (Norwegian Institute of International Affairs) & Fafo 2001, 'Gendering human security: from marginalisation to the integration of women in peace-building – recommendations for policy and practice from the NUPI-Fafo Forum on Gender Relations in Post-Conflict Transitions', *Fafo-report 352/NUPI-report 261*, www.fafo.no/pub/rapp/352/352.pdf (accessed 24 August 2011).

Nzomo, M 2002, 'Gender, governance and conflicts in Africa', *DPMF Workshop and Conference Proceedings*, www.dpmf.org/images/gender-maria.htm (accessed 24 August 2011).

Ogunsanya, K 2007, 'Women transforming conflicts in Africa: descriptive studies from Burundi, Cote d'Ivoire, Sierra Leone, South Africa and Sudan', *ACCORD Occasional Paper Series* 2(3).

Otto D. 2006, 'Lost in translation: re-scripting the sexed subject of international human rights law' in A Orford (ed.), *International law and its others*, Cambridge University Press, Cambridge, cited in Charlesworth 2008.

Pham, JP 2004, 'Lazarus rising: civil society and Sierra Leone's return from the grave', *The International Journal of Not-for-Profit Law* 7(1), November, www.icnl.org/knowledge/ijnl/vol7iss1/art_2.htm#_edn5 (accessed 22 August 2011).

Powley, E 2003, *Strengthening governance: the role of women in Rwanda's transition*, Hunt Alternatives Fund, Washington, DC.

—— 2006, 'Rwanda: the impact of women legislators on policy outcomes affecting children and families', background paper for United Nations Children's Fund 2006, *The State of the World's Children 2007*, UNICEF, New York.

Pulea, M 1985, 'Customary law relating to the environment: South Pacific region – an overview', South Pacific Commission, New Caledonia, cited in Corrin 2008.

Sainsbury, D 2004, 'Women's political representation in Sweden: discursive politics and institutional presence', *Scandinavian Political Studies* 27(1): 65–87.

Saovana-Spriggs, R 2007, 'Gender and peace: Bougainvillean women, matriliny, and the peace process', PhD dissertation, Australian National University, Canberra.

Sørensen, BR 1998, 'Women and post-conflict reconstruction: issues and sources', *WSP Occasional Paper* 3, Programme for Strategic and International Security Studies, United Nations Research Institute for Social Development.

UNAMA (United Nations Assistance Mission in Afghanistan) & OHCHR (Office of the High Commissioner for Human Rights) 2010, 'Harmful traditional practices and implementation of the Law on Elimination of Violence against Women in Afghanistan', UNAMA, Kabul and OHCHR, Geneva, 9 December, www.afghan-web.com/woman/harmful_traditions.pdf (accessed 22 August 2011).

UNICEF (United Nations Children's Fund) 2005. 'Humanitarian situation report,' UNICEF, New York, August, cited in International Crisis Group 2006.

UNIFEM (United Nations Development Fund for Women) 2002, 'Women, war and peace: the independent experts' assessment on the impact of armed conflict on women and women's role in peacebuilding', UNIFEM, New York.

—— 2004, *Getting it right, doing it right: gender and disarmament, demobilization and reintegration*, UNIFEM, New York, www.unifem.org/attachments/products/Getting_it_Right__Doing_it_Right.pdf (accessed 8 December 2010).

—— 2006, 'Beyond numbers: supporting women's political participation and promoting gender equality in post-conflict governance in Africa – a review of the role of the United Nations Development Fund for Women', UNIFEM, New York.

United Nations 2004, 'Statement by the President of the Security Council', S/PRST/2004/40, 28 October, www.un.org/womenwatch/ods/S-PRST-2004-40-E.pdf (accessed 22 August 2011).

—— 2005, 'Statement by the President of the Security Council', S/PRST/2005/52, 27 October, www.un.org/womenwatch/ods/S-PRST-2005-52-E.pdf (accessed 22 August 2011).

—— 2010, 'Women and peace and security: report of the Secretary-General', United Nations Security Council, 2/2010/498, 28 September, daccess-dds-ny.un.org/doc/UNDOC/GEN/N10/540/24/PDF/N1054024.pdf?OpenElement (accessed 6 December 2010).

United Nations Department of Peacekeeping Operations/Department of Field Support-Department of Political Affairs 2007, 'DPKO DFS-DPA Joint guidelines on enhancing the role of women in post-conflict electoral processes', Gabriele Russo, New York, October, cited in Butler et al. 2010.

Webber, K & Johnson H 2008, 'Women, peace building and political inclusion: a case study from Solomon Islands', *Hecate* 34(2): 83–99.

ANNEX: United Nations Security Council Resolution 1325

Adopted by the Security Council at its 4213th meeting, on 31 October 2000

The Security Council,

Recalling its resolutions 1261 (1999) of 25 August 1999, 1265 (1999) of 17 September 1999, 1296 (2000) of 19 April 2000 and 1314 (2000) of 11 August 2000, as well as relevant statements of its President and *recalling also* the statement of its President to the press on the occasion of the United Nations Day for Women's Rights and International Peace (International Women's Day) of 8 March 2000 (SC/6816),

Recalling also the commitments of the Beijing Declaration and Platform for Action (A/52/231) as well as those contained in the outcome document of the twenty-third Special Session of the United Nations General Assembly entitled "Women 2000: Gender Equality, Development and Peace for the twenty-first century" (A/S-23/10/Rev.1), in particular those concerning women and armed conflict,

Bearing in mind the purposes and principles of the Charter of the United Nations and the primary responsibility of the Security Council under the Charter for the maintenance of international peace and security,

Expressing concern that civilians, particularly women and children, account for the vast majority of those adversely affected by armed conflict, including as refugees and internally displaced persons, and increasingly are targeted by combatants and armed elements, and *recognizing* the consequent impact this has on durable peace and reconciliation,

Reaffirming the important role of women in the prevention and resolution of conflicts and in peace-building, and *stressing* the importance of their equal participation and full involvement in all efforts for the maintenance and promotion of peace and security, and the need to increase their role in decision- making with regard to conflict prevention and resolution,

Reaffirming also the need to implement fully international humanitarian and human rights law that protects the rights of women and girls during and after conflicts,

Emphasizing the need for all parties to ensure that mine clearance and mine awareness programmes take into account the special needs of women and girls,

Recognizing the urgent need to mainstream a gender perspective into peacekeeping operations, and in this regard *noting* the Windhoek Declaration and the Namibia Plan of Action on Mainstreaming a Gender Perspective in Multidimensional Peace Support Operations (S/2000/693),

Recognizing also the importance of the recommendation contained in the statement of its President to the press of 8 March 2000 for specialized training for all peacekeeping personnel on the protection, special needs and human rights of women and children in conflict situations,

Recognizing that an understanding of the impact of armed conflict on women and girls, effective institutional arrangements to guarantee their protection and full participation in the peace process can significantly contribute to the maintenance and promotion of international peace and security,

Noting the need to consolidate data on the impact of armed conflict on women and girls,

1. *Urges* Member States to ensure increased representation of women at all decision-making levels in national, regional and international institutions and mechanisms for the prevention, management, and resolution of conflict;

2. *Encourages* the Secretary-General to implement his strategic plan of action (A/49/587) calling for an increase in the participation of women at decision-making levels in conflict resolution and peace processes;

3. *Urges* the Secretary-General to appoint more women as special representatives and envoys to pursue good offices on his behalf, and in this regard *calls on* Member States to provide candidates to the Secretary-General, for inclusion in a regularly updated centralized roster;

4. *Further urges* the Secretary-General to seek to expand the role and contribution of women in United Nations field-based operations, and especially among military observers, civilian police, human rights and humanitarian personnel;

5. *Expresses* its willingness to incorporate a gender perspective into peacekeeping operations and *urges* the Secretary-General to ensure that, where appropriate, field operations include a gender component;

6. *Requests* the Secretary-General to provide to Member States training guidelines and materials on the protection, rights and the particular needs of women, as well as on the importance of involving women in all peacekeeping and peacebuilding measures, *invites* Member States to incorporate these elements as well as HIV/AIDS awareness training into their national training programmes for military and civilian police personnel in preparation for deployment and *further requests* the Secretary-General to ensure that civilian personnel of peacekeeping operations receive similar training;

7. *Urges* Member States to increase their voluntary financial, technical and logistical support for gender-sensitive training efforts, including those undertaken by relevant funds and programmes, inter alia, the United Nations

Fund for Women and United Nations Children's Fund, and by the United Nations High Commissioner for Refugees and other relevant bodies;

8. *Calls on* all actors involved, when negotiating and implementing peace agreements, to adopt a gender perspective, including, inter alia:

   (a) The special needs of women and girls during repatriation and resettlement and for rehabilitation, reintegration and post-conflict reconstruction;

   (b) Measures that support local women's peace initiatives and indigenous processes for conflict resolution, and that involve women in all of the implementation mechanisms of the peace agreements;

   (c) Measures that ensure the protection of and respect for human rights of women and girls, particularly as they relate to the constitution, the electoral system, the police and the judiciary;

9. *Calls upon* all parties to armed conflict to respect fully international law applicable to the rights and protection of women and girls as civilians, in particular the obligations applicable to them under the Geneva Conventions of 1949 and the Additional Protocols thereto of 1977, the Refugee Convention of 1951 and the Protocol thereto of 1967, the Convention on the Elimination of All Forms of Discrimination against Women of 1979 and the Optional Protocol thereto of 1999 and the United Nations Convention on the Rights of the Child of 1989 and the two Optional Protocols thereto of 25 May 2000, and to bear in mind the relevant provisions of the Rome Statute of the International Criminal Court;

10. *Calls on* all parties to armed conflict to take special measures to protect women and girls from gender-based violence, particularly rape and other forms of sexual abuse, and all other forms of violence in situations of armed conflict;

11. *Emphasizes* the responsibility of all States to put an end to impunity and to prosecute those responsible for genocide, crimes against humanity, war crimes including those relating to sexual violence against women and girls, and in this regard, stresses the need to exclude these crimes, where feasible from amnesty provisions;

12. *Calls upon* all parties to armed conflict to respect the civilian and humanitarian character of refugee camps and settlements, and to take into account the particular needs of women and girls, including in their design, and recalls its resolution 1208 (1998) of 19 November 1998;

13. *Encourages* all those involved in the planning for disarmament, demobilization and reintegration to consider the different needs of female and male ex-combatants and to take into account the needs of their dependants;

14. *Reaffirms* its readiness, whenever measures are adopted under Article 41 of the Charter of the United Nations, to give consideration to their potential impact on the civilian population, bearing in mind the special needs of women and girls, in order to consider appropriate humanitarian exemptions;

15. *Expresses* its willingness to ensure that Security Council missions take into account gender considerations and the rights of women, including through consultation with local and international women's groups;

16. *Invites* the Secretary-General to carry out a study on the impact of armed conflict on women and girls, the role of women in peace-building and the gender dimensions of peace processes and conflict resolution, and *further invites* him to submit a report to the Security Council on the results of this study and to make this available to all Member States of the United Nations;

17. *Requests* the Secretary-General, where appropriate, to include in his reporting to the Security Council, progress on gender mainstreaming throughout peace-keeping missions and all other aspects relating to women and girls;

18. *Decides* to remain actively seized of the matter.